Darwin's
Dead Ruse

Darwin's Dead Ruse

John Martin

DARWIN'S DEAD RUSE

iUniverse books may be ordered through booksellers or by contacting:

iUniverse
1663 Liberty Drive
Bloomington, IN 47403
www.iuniverse.com
844-349-9409

ISBN: 978-1-6632-5755-0 (sc)
ISBN: 978-1-6632-5754-3 (e)

Library of Congress Control Number: 2023920796

Print information available on the last page.

iUniverse rev. date: 11/22/2023

In 1849, the California gold rush started. The Sierra Nevada mountains were searched by prospectors looking for gold. A flower was noticed, it was very fragrant at night. It was Mimulus Moscata, which has the common name of; Monkey Musk flower. Because of its strong fragrance at night, someone sent seeds back home to

Europe. It began to be grown by gardeners in Great Britain, Germany, and possibly other countries. Then, in 1917 it stopped being fragrant. This is proof against Darwin's Entirely Atheistic Doctrine of Random, Unguided Species Evolution. Known by its acronym: D.E.A.D. R.U.S.E. To explain; Atheist scientist say that there are two ways that a plant changes. Natural selection, and human selection. In natural selection, a mutation might happen and, as example, one plant might become fragrance free. This would not help it reproduce as it would attract less

attention from pollinating insects. Now, in the case of human selection, humans would select the most fragrant flowers to grow. Any fragrance free plants would not be grown. In the case of the Monkey Musk flower, after the flowers became unfragrant, wild stocks of the flower were searched for, and it was discovered that all the plants in the wild had become fragrance free also. I believe that God had decided to give mankind an easy to understand example of how the D.E.A.D. R.U.S.E. does not work. Perhaps, because world war one caused so many young men

to die, while still deluded by D.E.A.D. R.U.S.E. the reader might ask; why the Monkey Musk flower? Wouldn't it be more clear if some other kind of plant had been changed? Not too many people were growing the Monkey Musk flower. But, other plants (as example; Watermelons), were grown by thousands of farmers. So, if all the watermelons in the world began producing small, black, dry, melons, people would know all over the world, right away. However, if this happened, there would be much unhappiness. Farmers would lose their livelihood,

people would miss eating watermelon. While by comparison, gardeners who grow a fragrant flower, are not doing so expecting a profit. God is good. God is smart.

To make it easy on the reader, I will now, in a generic way, explain what NOT to believe. I hope that this makes it easier to know what to believe. Analogies follow. Begin story number one:

One day an inventor, who had many great inventions, like an improvement on the ball bearing, that uses magnetic and anti-magnetic repulsion (to have no friction), decided to have a party, and show the public his inventions. He told his employees of the plan, and asked them to invite people to attend on the day of

the party. Later, on the day of the party, he saw one employee was accompanied by two women who looked scared. He asked the employee why the women looked scared. The employee answered; Oh, that's because I told them that I would kill them if they didn't come with me. So that, I could get the one hour of overtime. The boss then said: You're fired! Go to hell!

Question to the ready: Would you have the same reaction? God is not pathetic. Conversion by the sword, (if approved by a religion's founder), indicates that the religion is a false religion.

Analogy story number two:

There was an evil man named Elron Malfeasant. He wanted to rule the world. He decided to make a fake religion of war, so that he could get soldiers to fight and die for him. He knew that young men wanted sex most of all. He realized that he could lie and claim that; if they died fighting, they could have a large harem of beautiful young women, in the afterlife. He came up with a plan. He would use some other religious history book, but add his lies to it. So, he wrote that; if you

fought and died for his wars, you received 48 wives and lived in a paradise afterlife. To make it easier to get converts, he wrote that it was approved to kill anyone who refused to accept this (false) religion. He decided to make it seem reasonable, so, one had four opportunities to convert, but then, if they refused, it was approved to execute the person. Time passed, and the religion was getting converts, until they met someone who pointed out to the other townspeople that this was a religion of war, and war was a cause of terrible suffering and misery. And God

wants people to be happy, so, a religion of war is clearly untrue. He also gave his opinion, that God is not pathetic, and doesn't need people who are not truly converts, just pretenders, because they know they might be murdered, if they don't follow orders. The townspeople then told Malfeasant's agent to get lost. The agent went back to Malfeasant, and told him about what had happened. Malfeasant thought about it, and decided on a plan; in his fake book, he would add two sentences; one would state: This is a religion of peace. The other sentence: God

is great. This would be at the beginning of the book. This would counteract the evidence that his false religion was a religion of war. Malfeasant believed that these two sentences would be enough to trick most people.

Malfeasant took control of a large island. Foreigners wanted to buy the colored sand that they called lithium. Malfeasant invited 100,000 men and 100,000 women to apply for jobs washing the sand. Soon, the island was fully staffed. Malfeasant told the men that they were allowed four wives. He told them where the marriage licenses were to be purchased. Then, he waited. The island was one hundred miles offshore. After seven months, he returned to the island. He went to the marriage license office and asked; how many men had married? And, to how many women?

Malfeasant was informed that twenty thousand and one men had married. All had married three wives each. Malfeasant did the math; twenty times three equals sixty. And one hundred minus sixty equals forty. So, there were approximately forty thousand single women left on the island. And approximately eighty thousand single men. Malfeasant was pleased. This serves well the religion of war. He made a speech to the men on the island. He invited them to join the military, as we had to invade the island of Boobiesdroop. Right away, men lined up

to join the army. After a week, Malfeasant was pleased with his plan to allow and encourage men to have four wives. This will make the remaining single men more desperate, and more willing to join the army, with opportunities to rape the enemy's women.

A complicated world does not just happen by chance. The Earth is just far enough away from the sun, so, things are not burned. And just close enough, so, plants can grow. If the distance between the sun and the earth was one half of one percent closer, the earth would be a boiled, lifeless wasteland. On the other hand, if the earth was one half of one percent further away from the sun, the earth would be an icy frozen lifeless world. Thank God that the distance is just right for life on earth. One more point: The sun gives off dangerous radiation, as well as the

sunlight plants need. I will use the word x-rays, for this description, although there is a spectrum of radiation given off by the sun. X-rays injure and kill living things, both plants and animals. So, I believe that when God created the earth, a screen was installed to screen out the x-rays. The screen is called Van Allen belts. It is named that because it was discovered by James Van Allen. The Van Allen belts are an electromagnetic screen that blocks most of the x-rays from hitting plants and animals on the surface of the earth. I believe that this is

more proof of creation. I do not believe that Van Allen belts happened by chance coincidence. Are there any other planets that have Van Allen belts? Why not?

Another complicated part of animal life is instinct. Instinct is an innate knowledge of what to do. A researcher did an experiment on weaver birds. Weaver birds are a species of bird that make their nest by weaving plant fibers together in a complicated way, unlike most bird's nests of stacked twigs. The researcher built an aviary cage. He kept it free of any birds, and then collected some eggs of weaver birds. He put the eggs in an incubator. After the eggs hatched, he hand fed the chicks. The baby chicks never saw or heard any adult weaver bird. Later, after

the birds had grown into adulthood, they made the intricately woven nest, because they have instinct. The birds had never seen a nest constructed. All animals have instinct, and basically know what to do. People do not have many instincts. One that people have: When babies are newborn, if pressed on the cheek, the baby turns his or her face towards the pressed side. This helps the baby find the Mother's nipple.

The author is a Baptist. You are invited to visit the Baptist Christian church near to where you live.